FOLENS HISTORY

THE ROMAN EMPIRE

RESOURCE BOOK

CAROLE BROWN

INTRODUCTION

This teacher-resource book is designed to support and extend *The Roman Empire*, one of five Folens core text books which fulfil all the Attainment Targets of the National Curriculum Key Stage 3 History.

All Folens' history books aim to help pupils study history through the use and interpretation of evidence. Pupils are encouraged to examine primary and secondary evidence and to put together their own ideas about what might have happened.

Activities create opportunities for:

- the development of the ability to describe and explain historical change and cause, and analyse different features of historical situations;
- the development of the ability to understand interpretation of history;
- the development of pupils' ability to acquire evidence from historical sources, and form judgements about their reliability and value.

Such activities relate directly to the three Attainment Targets set out for National Curriculum history. In addition a matrix is included at the end of this book in order that teachers may identify which Attainment Targets are being met by each Unit.

The majority of Units in this Resource Book can be photocopied for use in the classroom. They are designed to encourage the active involvement of pupils and the study of history. It is also hoped that at the time when 'paper pushing' threatens to take over, teachers will find these Units ease the load of lesson preparation.

Folens
COPYMASTER

Illustrations by Melissa Mee.

First published 1991 by Folens Limited, Dunstable and Dublin.

ISBN 1 85276164-4

Folens Limited. Apex Business Centre, Boscombe Road, Dunstable, LU5 4RL, England.

Printed by Ashford Colour Press.

CONTENTS

1. THE BIRTH OF THE ROMAN EMPIRE

Aim To establish the prior knowledge of pupils.

Introduction The two activities in this unit should be undertaken before Unit 1 in *The Roman Empire*. The activities are designed to draw on pupils' knowledge, particularly that developed in Key Stage 2.

Resource Photocopiable pupil resource sheet page 5.

ACTIVITY

Objective: that pupils should brainstorm all their ideas about the Romans and their achievements.
Skills: cooperative learning; communication; brainstorming; factual recall.

Organisation Pupils should be divided into small groups of four or five. However, if pupils are unfamiliar with brainstorming then the activity could be teacher led.

Approach

- Explain the rules of brainstorming, i.e. anyone can make a contribution; no one may question a contribution; all ideas are of value and will be accepted.
- If pupils are working in small groups they should elect a scribe.
- Ask pupils to think back over the history they did in primary school about the Romans.
- Then either give out the spider diagram on page 5 and ask pupils to complete it by brainstorming what they can remember, or draw the spider diagram on the blackboard and ask pupils to call out their ideas.
- If the activity is teacher led, pupils can write up the brainstorm on their own spider diagram.
- As ideas begin to dry up, ask pupils to categorise the information. This may require some explanation. The best way of categorisation is to ring related ideas, using a separate colour chalk or crayon for each category.
- The following categories should emerge: everyday life; housing; trade; the army; the empire; work; leisure; etc.

ACTIVITY

Objective: that pupils should identify evidence from Roman times.
Skills: cooperative learning; communication; problem-solving.

Organisation Divide class into pairs or small groups of three or four. Each group should have paper on which to write their ideas, and the Clue Sheet from page 5.

Approach

- Tell pupils they are historians about to start investigating the Romans.
- They are to make a list of all the evidence they would use.
- The Clue Sheet from page 5 will help them.

Debrief *Allow time for discussion about these activities. Did the groups have any problems brainstorming? What were these problems? Emphasise that they already have a lot of knowledge about the Romans.*

THE ROMANS AND THEIR ACHIEVEMENTS

What can you remember about the Romans?

Look for clues!

Places you have visited or television programmes you have seen.

Things the Romans may have left behind.

Countries or places connected with the Romans.

2. THE PUNIC WARS

Aim To develop pupils' knowledge of chronology.

Introduction These activities are designed to be undertaken as an introduction to Unit 2 in *The Roman Empire*.

Resource Photocopiable resource sheet page 7, which should be cut into separate cards. It is advisable to place each pack in a separate envelope.

ACTIVITY

Objective: that pupils should sequence the cards in the correct chronological order.
Skills: communication; problem-solving; chronology.

Organisation Pupils should work in pairs. If each pair of pupils can work at a separate table or desk it helps prevent cards becoming mixed. The cards are printed in chronological order. Please mix before giving to pupils.

Approach

- ▼ Some discussion regarding the meaning of chronology helps pupils understand the aim of this activity.
- ▼ It is also helpful to ask pupils what clues they might use when trying to sequence cards which do not have a date. As this may be the first sequencing exercise pupils have undertaken, most cards do have a date.
- ▼ Some explanation of BC and the way in which these dates operate will also be needed.

Debrief *Spend some time discussing the problems which arose during the activity.*

ACTIVITY

Objective: that pupils should place the events of the Punic Wars on a time line.
Skills: chronology; sequencing.

Organisation Pupils could work individually or in pairs.

Approach

- ▼ If this is the first time that pupils have undertaken time-line work, then a teacher-led activity may prove the most productive.
- ▼ Pupils can use the sequence cards from page 7 as well as Unit 2 in *The Roman Empire*.
- ▼ It will be necessary to establish a scale which stretches from 246 to 146 BC.

266 ***BC.*** *Rome controlled the whole of Italy.*

Carthage was a city whose people built a large empire ***3rd Century BC.***

The First Punic War ***264 BC.*** *Rome helped Sicily drive out the Carthaginians.*

The Romans built warships and chased the Carthaginians back to Carthage.

241 BC. *The Romans defeated the Carthaginians.*

The Second Punic War ***218 BC.*** *Hannibal, a Carthaginian, crossed the Alps.*

Wild tribes rolled boulders on to Hannibal and his men.

Hannibal had 50 000 men. By the time he reached Italy only 26 000 were still alive.

At Cannae ***216 BC.*** *Hannibal beat the Romans.*

At Zama in ***202 BC.*** *the Romans beat Hannibal.*

Hannibal was captured, but took poison and died.

The Third Punic War ***149 BC.*** *Romans attacked and defeated the Carthaginians, who were sold into slavery.*

3. GROWTH OF THE EMPIRE

Aim

That pupils should describe and interpret visual evidence.

Introduction

This exercise can be used before or after pupils have studied Unit 3 in *The Roman Empire*.

Resource

Photocopiable resource sheet page 9 and slides, if you can obtain them, showing remains of the Roman Empire. For example, Hadrian's Wall; Rome; Pompeii; France; North Africa. A slide projector and a screen will also be required.

ACTIVITY

Objective: that pupils should describe each slide in detail and explain what can be learned about the Romans from the slide.
Skills: observation; interpretation of pictorial evidence; communication.

Organisation

It is important that only a small number of slides are used. If this type of exercise is new to pupils, then it will be more successful if teacher led. Once the skills of observation and interpretation have been learned then the exercise could be undertaken by a small group, with occasional teacher guidance. Pupils should be seated in small groups so that discussion and note-taking can take place.

Approach

- Pupils should be given the photocopiable resource sheet, which will help them to keep well organised notes.
- The procedure for each slide:
  - It should be stressed to pupils that one needs to learn to 'read' pictorial evidence as one would learn to read a book. Therefore, pupils should begin in the top left-hand corner of the slide and work downwards, describing what they can see to a partner.
  - These observations can then be shared with the whole group. The quickest way of achieving this is for one group to describe the top part of the slide, then another group to present observations on the next section and so on. Once it has been established that pupils are describing in detail, the sharing of observations with the whole class can be omitted.
  - Pupils should then write up their description in the column headed 'Observations'. This can be done in numbered points.
  - Pupils should now be asked to interpret the slide. Stress that such interpretations are only our ideas and as such are provisional. Further evidence is needed to support our interpretations. Some explanation about the meaning of interpretation will be required. Perhaps the easiest way of doing this is to say that pupils are going to explain what they can learn about the Romans from the slide. This may need stimulation from the teacher through the use of questions. For example, what skills did the Romans need to build Hadrian's Wall? What tools and materials would be needed? What sort of workforce? What problems might they have faced? After discussion these ideas can be written down in the 'Interpretation' column.

Debrief

Spend time discussing any problems which arose during the exercise. Did the pupils enjoy it? How could it be improved?

PHOTOCOPIABLE

THE GROWTH OF THE ROMAN EMPIRE

SLIDE NUMBER	OBSERVATIONS	INTERPRETATION
1		
2		
3		
4		
5		

PHOTOCOPIABLE

4. ROMAN LAW AND CITIZENSHIP

NOW

Using Unit 4 from *The Roman Empire* make your own notes or drawings under the headings below.

Citizens' Rights

Punishments for Citizens

Punishments for Slaves

Consuls:

Government Officials

Senate:

Popular Assembly:

5. JULIUS CAESAR

Aim

That pupils should find out about the life of Julius Caesar.

Introduction

This activity should be undertaken before pupils begin Unit 5 in *The Roman Empire*.

Resources

The briefing notes on page 13 Unit 5 in *The Roman Empire*. A white sheet to use as a toga, together with flat leather sandals. Someone to play the role of Caesar!

ACTIVITY

Objective: that pupils should ask questions about Julius Caesar.
Skills: question formulation; note-taking; listening.

Organisation

Pupils will need exercise books and should sit in a semicircle. One chair should be placed at the open end of the circle for the visitor.

Approach

▼ It should be explained that a visitor who knows a great deal about life in Roman times is about to arrive.
▼ The group has ten minutes to prepare questions.
▼ Suggest that the answers should be recorded in the form of a spider diagram. Try to elicit suggestions for headings from the pupils, although the headings from the teacher's resource sheet can be used. Caesar's name and dates will be entered in the centre of the diagram.
▼ Then either leave the room and reappear in role or collect the 'visitor'.
▼ At the end of the visit leave the room, then reappear as yourself for the debrief.

Clues to Success

* Do maintain your role throughout. You can reprimand in role if need be; although in the author's experience, pupils are so fascinated and suspend disbelief so quickly that few problems arise.
* If they ask how you can still be alive, explain that you woke after a long sleep (death) and found yourself in their time. Claim loss of memory if there are questions you can't answer!
* Do ask questions about things around you which Caesar would not have seen. For example: lights, pens, boys and girls being educated together, clothing, etc.

Follow-up

● *Notes can be written up and illustrated.*
● *A diary entry could be produced.*
● *Photographs could be taken or a video made of the visit.*

Debrief

Ask pupils to assess the lesson. Did they enjoy it? What did they learn?
Ask them to assess the reliability of the teacher as evidence. Where had the information been found?

JULIUS CAESAR c102BC - 44BC

Early Life and Background

Born into a noble family, although most of the family wealth had been lost. However, Caesar was still given a good education. Married at the age of 17 years. Joined the army. Became well known in 80 BC at Battle of Mitylene when he saved the life of another soldier. c78 BC returned to Rome and made a career as a lawyer.

Events

In his twenties went to Rhodes to improve his command of speaking in public. Captured by pirates, who demanded a ransom. Became very friendly with pirates and joined in their sport and games. Once his ransom was paid and he was released, Caesar hired ships, returned to the pirates and crucified each one. He then recovered the ransom money.

Life in Rome

Caesar then returned to Rome. General information about life in Rome could be given at this point. Such items as baths, shops, aqueducts, sewers, slaves and buildings could be covered. (See Folen's *The Roman Empire* Units 14, 15, 17 and 21.)

Political Career

68 BC appointed one of the 20 Roman quaestors (financial officers). This gave him a seat in the Senate. Spent some time as a successful governor of Spain.

60 BC returned to Rome and was chosen by Pompey to become Consul with him.

58-49 BC after his year as Consul Caesar applied to become Governor of Gaul. This was a very difficult post, but Caesar succeeded in extending the Roman Empire to include all of modern day France plus Belgium and parts of the Netherlands.

55 and 54 BC Caesar landed in Britain and marched as far as the Thames. He had to return to Gaul as there was always the danger of uprisings there.

49 BC Pompey was losing power in Rome. Caesar marched to Rome with his men and entered in triumph. The next five years were spent defeating Pompey and his sons. Then Caesar became the first Emperor of Rome and restored law and order to the capital.

Caesar the Soldier

Caesar had great success in motivating his men, mainly because he always fought with them near the front lines. He marched and ate with his men. He slept outside his tent with them in the open. They both feared and respected him. Caesar had also realised that the way to power in Rome was through the army.

Death of Caesar

Although Caesar was emperor, people plotted his death. It took place on the Ides of March - 15th March 44 BC Caesar's wife dreamed of the plot and begged him not to attend the Senate, but he insisted on going. People in the streets also warned him of danger, but he continued. After he had taken his seat in the Senate he was attacked and murdered by a group of young men, many of whom Caesar had befriended.

Other Achievements

Caesar reformed the calendar - July is named after him; established public libraries; reduced tax for ordinary people; set up local authorities in towns called municipia; he encouraged ex-soldiers to establish colonies throughout the empire; he planned many buildings in Rome; developed the first system of coinage to carry the ruler's portrait.

6. THE ROMAN ARMY

The Roman Empire depended on a strong army to defend it. During the time of the Empire men volunteered to become soldiers. They usually agreed to become a soldier for 20 years. They were well paid and could work their way up through the ranks. To become a legionary, men had to be Roman citizens and at least 1.74 metres tall.

New volunteers for the Roman army were taken to training camps. There they were taught to march, ride horses, to swim and fight. However, soldiers also had to learn other skills, such as road and bridge building. The legionary was a foot soldier, but there were also soldiers on horseback called cavalry.

In battle soldiers used catapults, spears and arrows, as well as their swords and javelins. They also built large siege towers and made long ladders to help them climb walls.

At the end of the 20 years they were given a pension, together with a piece of land on which to build a villa.

Answer these questions in your note book.

- ▼ Why did the Empire need a strong army?
- ▼ What qualifications did men need to join the army?
- ▼ Describe the training of soldiers.
- ▼ Why do you think the sandals had iron studs?
- ▼ What was used to make the armour?
- ▼ What did soldiers have to do as well as fight?
- ▼ What was the legionary's reward at the end of 20 years' service?

NOW **Write these labels on the drawing of the legionary in the correct places.**

- *Leather sandals with iron studs on the soles.*
- *Iron helmet lined with leather, to protect head and neck.*
- *Short iron sword with a bone handle.*
- *Shield made from wood and covered with leather.*
- *Javelin with wooden shaft and iron head.*
- *Armour made from iron plates and backed with leather.*
- *Belt made from metal plates, with an apron of metal plates hanging from it.*
- *Short tunic made from hard leather.*

7. CLAUDIUS

Aim

To introduce pupils to the problems and decisions faced by the Romans.

Introduction

The two activities in this section should be undertaken before Unit 7 in *The Roman Empire.*

Resources

Photocopiable pupil resource sheet page 15. Notebooks and pens.

ACTIVITY

Objective: that pupils should develop an understanding of the factors which influenced the Roman decision to invade Britain.
Skills: communication; problem-solving; decision-making; listening.

Organisation

Pupils should be seated in groups of 4 - 6.

Approach

- ▼ The teacher as Claudius should set the scene. A possible script might be: *"Members of the senate, I Claudius have called you here to discuss the possible invasion of Britannia. I want each group to decide whether or not we should invade. You must list the reasons to support your decision. I have here a fact file to help you reach your decision and a map of our Empire."*
- ▼ It is not necessary for the teacher to dress up, but it does help if the language is formalised.
- ▼ It should be stressed that each 'member of the Senate' should keep his/her own notes, but one person will be required to report back to the whole class.
- ▼ Issue Fact File 1 and the map and give a prescribed amount of time for discussion and decision making. About 10 minutes will be needed.
- ▼ Then issue Fact File 2, which provides information about the motives which Claudius might have had for an invasion. Pupils reconsider their decision and add to their list of supporting evidence.
- ▼ The selected reporter from each group gives their decision together with the supporting evidence. Claudius could keep score of those for and against.
- ▼ Hopefully the 'Senate' will decide to invade. However, should the opposite decision be made then Claudius can impose his decision.

ACTIVITY

Objective: that pupils should understand the problems which faced the Romans as a result of their decision to invade.
Skills: communication; problem-solving; decision-making; listening.

Organisation

Same groups as for previous activity.

Approach

- ▼ Ask each group to brainstorm a list of everything which they would need to do once the decision to invade had been made.
- ▼ The list can be drawn up on a large sheet of sugar paper and displayed on the wall. The groups can then move around reading the different lists.
- ▼ Differences and similarities can be drawn together by a teacher-led session.

Debrief

Discussion could centre around how the Fact Files influenced their decisions. Do pupils think that the activities were realistic? What did they learn about the motives of Claudius?

Further Work

- *Pupils could be given a limited time to find out what really happened using Unit 7 of The Roman Empire.*
- *A comparison of their own decision and their ideas about problems facing the Romans could then be made.*

FACT FILE 1 BRITANNIA

- Britannia is many hundreds of miles north of Rome.
- Roman ships have traded with the Britons since Julius Caesar crossed from Gaul to Britannia in 55 and 54 BC.
- We have traded silver goods, cloth and wine with the Britons.
- The Britons make excellent leather and woollen cloth. They also have many lead and tin mines.
- The climate of Britannia is cold, foggy and wet.
- Some of the tribes in the south of Britannia are friendly towards us.
- Most of the tribes further north are fierce and hostile (unfriendly).
- An invasion would be very expensive.

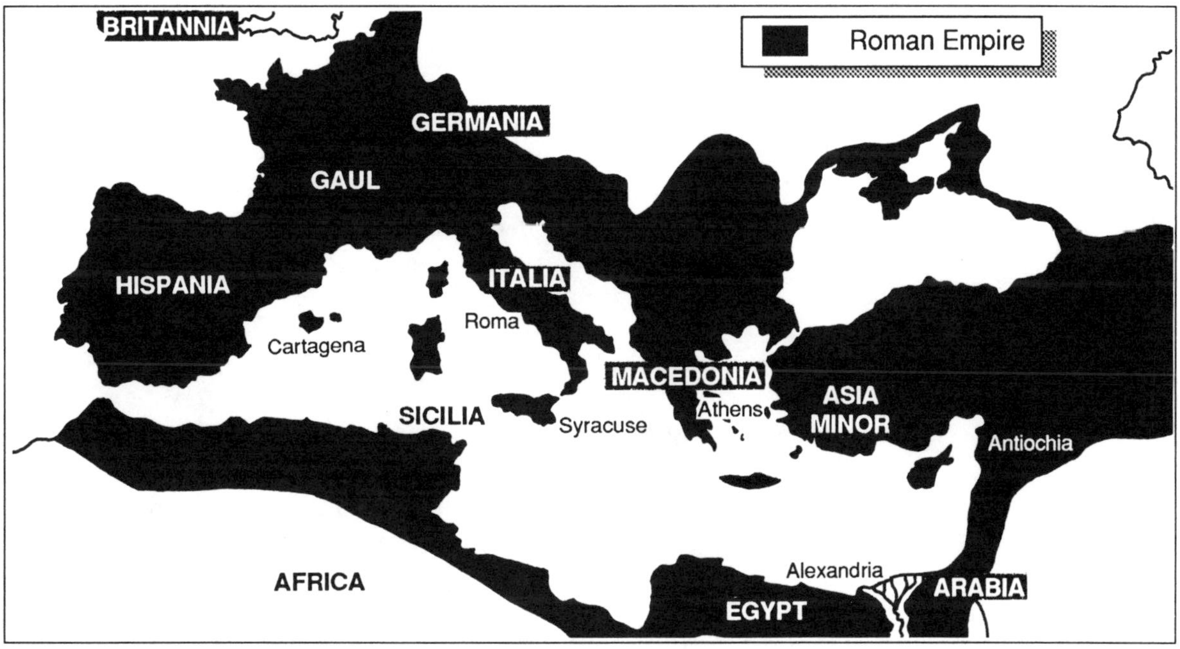

The Roman Empire in 41AD

FACT FILE 2 CLAUDIUS

- Claudius became emperor in 41 AD.
- He needed more support from the citizens of Rome if he was to stay in power.
- He was particularly worried that the army might turn against him.
- The Roman army were very restless. They needed a battle.
- Claudius was not very popular. He needed to improve his popularity with the people.

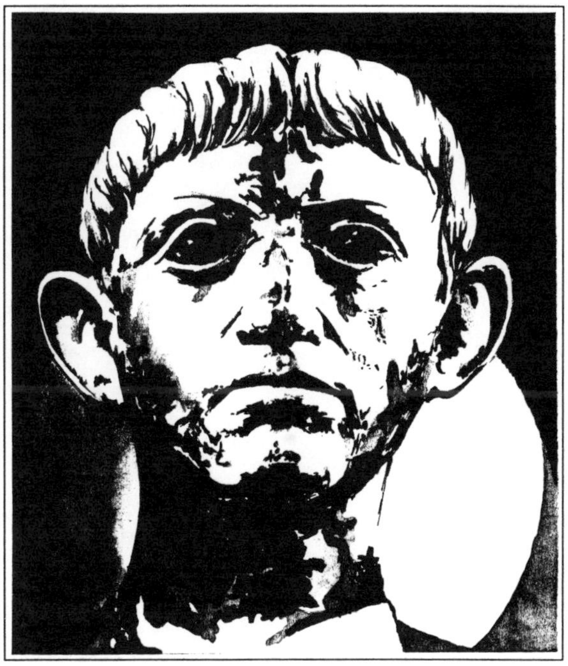

8. BOUDICA'S REBELLION

Aim

That pupils should further develop their knowledge of Boudica's rebellion by producing a radio news programme.

Resources

Pupil resource sheet page 17 and Unit 8 from *The Roman Empire*.
Optional: cassette recorder and cassette.

ACTIVITY

Objective: that pupils should present a radio news programme.
Skills: co-operative learning and working; information retrieval; planning and problem-solving; empathetic understanding.

Organisation

- ▼ Pupil resource sheet page 17 should be photocopied for each pupil.
- ▼ Divide the class into groups of 6 - 8.
- ▼ Each group should produce a script and every member of the group should have a copy. The scripts can be produced on word processors.
- ▼ A time limit for preparation should be agreed with the pupils.
- ▼ Programmes can all be recorded in one room. While one group records, the rest of the class become the studio audience. The words, *"Silence in the studio: 5-4-3-2-1 action!"* create the right atmosphere.

Approach

- ▼ This activity should be undertaken after pupils have completed Unit 8 in *The Roman Empire.*
- ▼ If pupils have not undertaken this type of exercise before, then it proves beneficial to:
  - listen to a radio news programme that includes an interview;
  - spend sometime practising interviews in pairs.
- ▼ Pupils should be encouraged to ask open questions during interviews.

Advantages

Pupils enjoy this exercise and it leads to good motivation. They also have reported that the exercise helps them to 'remember the facts.'

Clues to Success

Some pupils do feel very self-conscious about recording when others are watching and listening. This could be overcome by providing additional cassette recorders and some groups retiring to another room to complete their recording.

RADIO NEWS

BOUDICA'S REBELLION

You are used to listening to radio and watching television. Both these inventions make it very easy to transmit news quickly over long distances. In Roman times radio and television had not been invented and news travelled very slowly - usually at the speed of the fastest runner or horseman! In this exercise you are going to imagine that radio had been invented in Roman times and you are a news presenter giving your view of Boudica's Rebellion.

- Work in a group of 6 - 8 people.
- Read Unit 8 in *The Roman Empire* and complete the activities.
- You will need the following characters for your news broadcast:
  the news reader
  3 on-the-spot reporters (if you are short of people one person could play all 3 parts)
  Boudica and Suetonius
  you could also include interviews with a Roman soldier and a Briton if you wish.
- Plan the outline of your programme.
  Scene 1:
  News reader announces that a battle is taking place between Boudica and the Roman Governor Suetonius. A description of Boudica and some background information can be given.
  Scene 2:
  On-the-spot reporter interviews Boudica. Could ask questions about why she has gone into battle with the Romans. The noise of battle could be heard in the background.
  Scene 3:
  On-the-spot reporter 2 interviews Suetonius. Questions could be asked about why he has chosen this site for the battle; how his men feel about facing a much larger army.
  Scene 4:
  On-the-spot reporter 3 describes the battle and how it ends.
  Scene 5:
  News reader in radio studio confirms the final result of the battle and closes the programme.
- Remember, every member of your group will need a script. You could write these on a word processor.
- Rehearse all the scenes carefully.
- When your group is ready, ask to record your programme on a cassette recorder.

- What people liked about your programme.
- How it could be improved.
- What you have learnt from this exercise. Will it help you remember the work on Boudica's rebellion?
- Taking the recording home for your parents to hear.

PHOTOCOPIABLE

9. A ROMAN KITCHEN

This is how a Roman kitchen in Britain might have looked during the 2nd century AD.

NOW

Using the descriptions below, label the items shown in the drawing.
Items found in a Roman kitchen.

- *The hearth - this was used to cook the food, but it also warmed the room.*
- *Fuel - wooden logs.*
- *Stone flags around hearth.*
- *Bracken for flooring.*
- *Clean bracken stored for future use.*
- *Cooking pots.*
- *Bowl and wooden spatula.*
- *Amphora - a large oval-shaped container for wine and oil. Sometimes used to store water.*
- *Iron frying pan.*
- *Loom for weaving cloth.*
- *Stone quern for grinding flour.*
- *Wooden preparation table.*

- What are the main differences between this kitchen and your own kitchen at home?

PHOTOCOPIABLE

ROMAN FOOD AND COOKING

Lettuce, parsnips, cabbage, radishes, turnips and watercress were grown. There were no potatoes in Roman times.

Below is more information about Roman food and cooking. The recipes below for poultry, with sauce and vegetables, followed by sweet bread will make a complete meal. Perhaps you could ask your Consumer Technology department if you could cook some of these recipes. The Sweet Bread recipe is very simple and really delicious!

Vegetables

Spiced Cabbage

1 small green cabbage.
2 - 3 small leeks
1 teaspoon liquamen (see recipe opposite)
1 tablespoon white wine
1 tablespoon oil
Dash of pepper
1 teaspoon caraway seeds
1 teaspoon ground cummin

Wash the cabbage then shred and boil. Do the same with the leeks. Mix other ingredients together as a dressing. When cabbage and leeks are tender place on a dish and pour dressing over.

Liquamen

This ingredient was found in many Roman recipes. It was used to add more flavour, rather as we might use Worcester sauce today. It was made by boiling together the following ingredients for 10 minutes:

1 glass of red wine
1 pint of water
75g salt
large pinch of oregano
2 or 3 anchovies

Then strain into a bottle.

Meat

Meat for use during the winter would be hung over the kitchen fire to smoke. During the summer fresh meat would be eaten. The main meal of the day was in the evening. It would be at this meal that meat was eaten.
Pork, duck, chicken, goose and hare were cooked, but Romans also enjoyed small birds like pigeon. Dormice stuffed with minced pork, pepper, herbs and pine nuts were a particular favourite.

Fish

Romans also enjoyed salmon, trout, pike, oysters and small shellfish.

Poultry

A sauce to accompany roast poultry

1 tablespoon of cooking oil
1 tablespoon of vinegar
1 glass of white wine
1 teaspoon of liquamen

Add to this liquid chopped celery, hazelnuts, almonds, honey; lovage and catmint to taste. Heat all the ingredients together. Make criss-cross cuts on the cooked bird and pour the sauce over.

Sweet Bread with Dates

Cut pieces of bread into cubes and soak in milk. Drain then fry in olive oil until golden brown. Pile into a dish, pour clear honey over and add chopped dates.

Desserts

These were usually quite simple. Fresh fruits, nuts and sweet cakes would be served. Honey was used to sweeten food.

Bread

Most households baked their own bread from corn flour which was ground in the home using a quern. Some loaves were spiced or flavoured with honey or cheese.

10. HADRIAN'S WALL

Aim

That pupils should record a site visit to some Roman remains.

Introduction

This unit contains ideas for on-site activities. The actual site chosen will depend on what is available in the part of the country in which you teach. Therefore the format of the pupil worksheet has been kept deliberately general and may require some adaptation for the site you have chosen.

The English, Welsh and Scottish Tourist Boards produce a small booklet entitled **'Discover Roman Britain'**. This gives details with maps of Roman sites throughout Britain. Write to: English Tourist Board, 4 Grosvenor Gardens, London SW1W ODU.

Possible Sites to Visit

Hadrian's Wall and its many forts and milecastles; villas; remains of Roman roads, Saxon shore forts, baths, settlements, cities - including Lincoln, York, London, Leicester. Excavation is still taking place on many of these sites.

Resources

Variable according to the activities undertaken, although the following are almost always useful: clipboards, pencils and clear plastic bags (for wet-weather problems); plain paper; cameras; tape measures.

Pre-visit Preparations

- The relevant body will need to be consulted and arrangements made.
- If you can't visit the site before the actual visit, do telephone the site warden who will help iron out problems. Do remember also to check the permitted teacher/pupil ratio as this often varies from site to site.

Pre-visit Activities

- Study any relevant units in *The Roman Empire;* show slides of the site to pupils; have a lesson based on sketching and labelling; practise drawing plans; look at the guide book.
- Inform parents of the visit. Send out relevant forms and details of clothing.
- Pupils should see and discuss any material which will be used on site.
- Pupils should work in small groups of 6 - 8, accompanied by an adult.
- Sites such as the forts on Hadrian's Wall are very large. Do let pupils explore, but focus the main work of each small group on one part of the site.

Possible On-Site Activities

- Pupils should be encouraged to describe the physical surroundings.
- Remains could be studied and sketches drawn to show their construction. The measurements could be paced out or measured accurately. Photographs could also be taken.
- A plan of the site or of a small part of the site could be drawn.
- Pupils could answer questions prepared on their pre-visit activities.
- Pupils could be provided with photographs of particular features of the site which they have to find, describe and interpret.
- Pupils could be asked to find evidence of and then investigate drainage systems, hypercaust systems, Roman art and mosaics, Roman engineering.
- A map could be provided with certain points highlighted. At each point pupils should make a sketch of what they find and identify what might have been built there.
- A list of statements about the site could be provided. Pupils should find evidence to support the truth or falsity of the statements. More able students could be asked to evaluate the site as historical evidence.

PHOTOCOPIABLE

SITE VISIT TO ROMAN REMAINS

You are about to begin an EXPLORATION of the site of some Roman remains. In order to do the work you will have to OBSERVE carefully and RECORD all the information to take back to school. You are also going to try to RECONSTRUCT how the site might have looked in the past.

WARNING!!
Remember these remains are between 1500 and 2000 years old. Try not to climb on the original remains.

LOOK AND OBSERVE

Look carefully at the site and its surroundings. Write a site description of the remains.
* Is it on a hill or flat land?
* Is it near a river, village or town?
* Is it close to trees or a road?
* Is it near any defence system like a ditch?
* Describe the building material used.

EXPLORATION

Before beginning your work EXPLORE the whole site with your group. Notice how much of the original building is left. Are the ruins quite high or very low on the ground? If you are looking at a building try to identify what it might have been or what part of the building you might be in. Now return to the entrance or to the area of the remains where your teacher told you to work.

NOW RECORD

Once you have reached the part of the site where you are going to work, complete the following:
- Draw a sketch and label building material and any special features.
- You could also take photographs if you have a camera.
- Draw a plan of the part of the remains you are studying.
- Take measurements of the remains. Use your stride or a tape measure.
- Mark the measurements on your plan.
- Make a list of any questions you want to ask about the remains.

RECONSTRUCTION

- Try to imagine how the remains might have looked when complete.
- Draw a sketch to show how it might have looked.
- Find somewhere to sit where you have a good view of the remains.
- Imagine you are back in Roman times. Write a story about the things you think you might have heard and seen.
  Look after all the information you have collected.

BACK AT SCHOOL

- Write up your work neatly and make a display.
- Use books to find out more about the site.
- Make a model of the site.
- Design a site trail for younger pupils to follow.
- Write a play about life at the site in Roman times.

PHOTOCOPIABLE

11. A ROMAN FORT

LOOK **Look carefully at the diagrams on these two pages.**

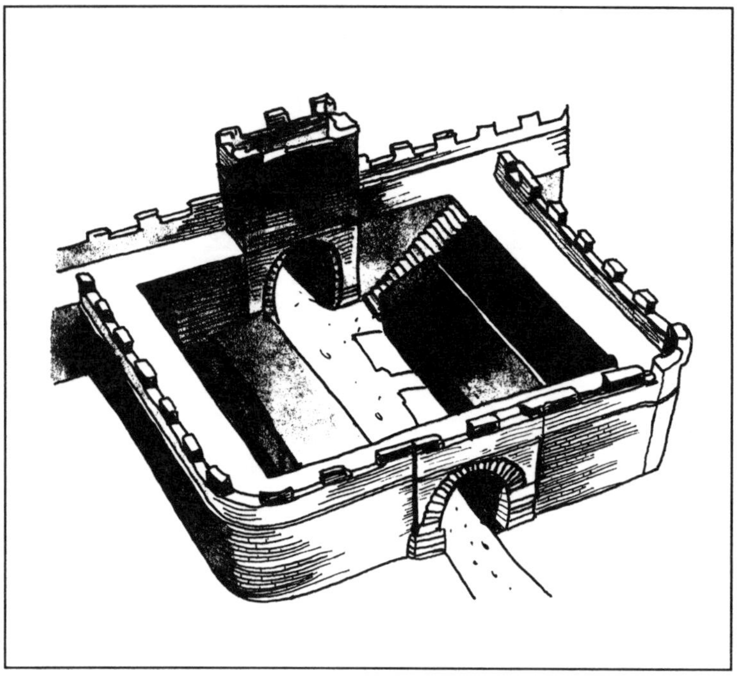

A stone milecastle

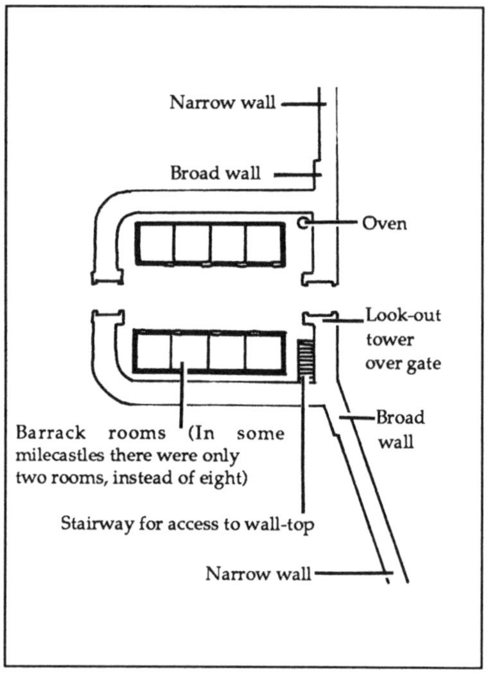

A plan of a stone milecastle

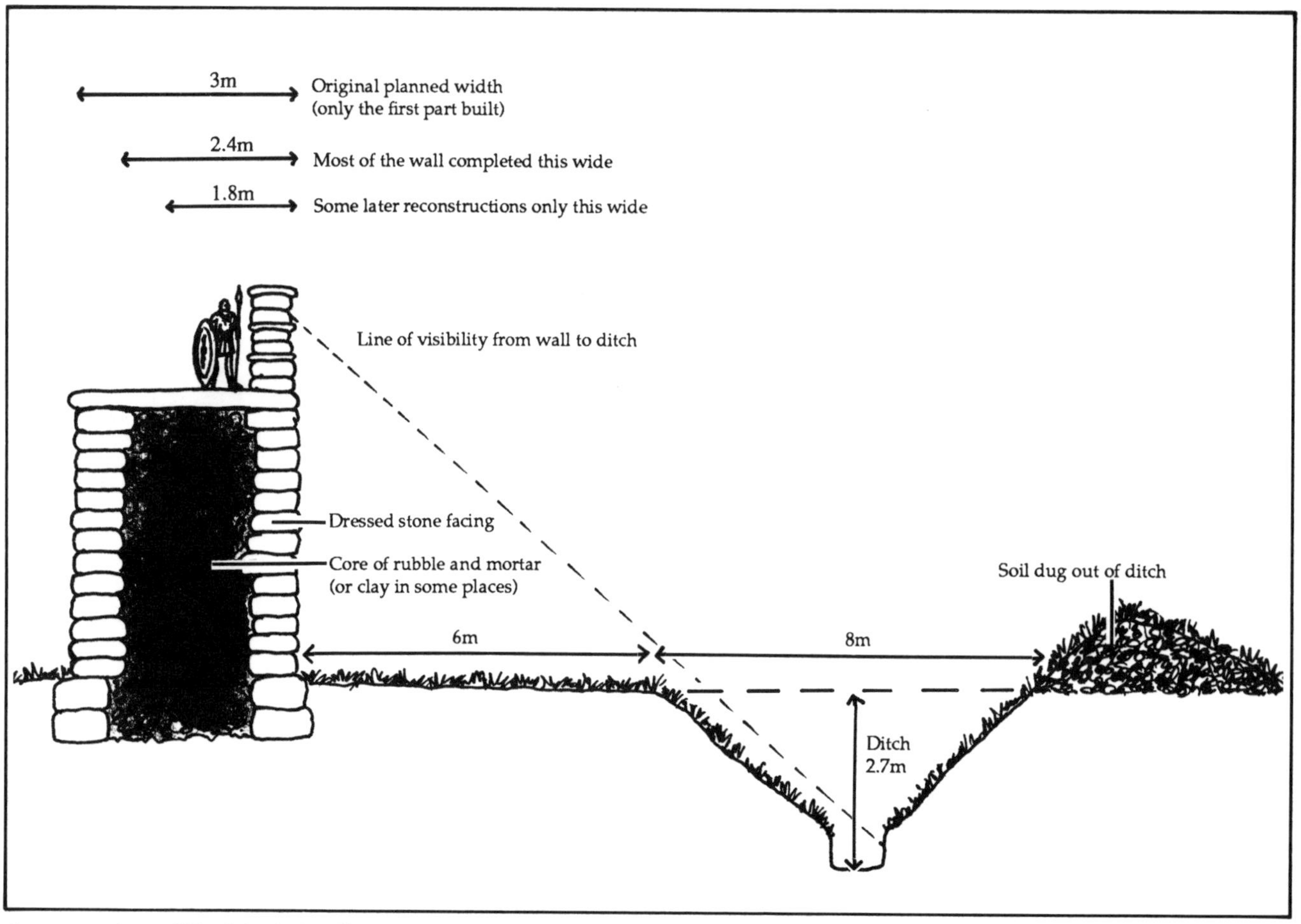

Cross section of Hadrian's Wall

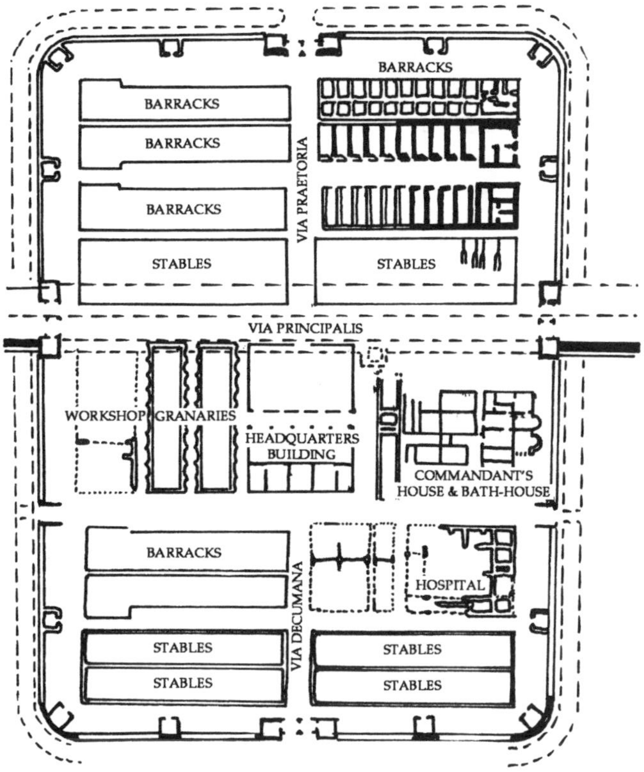

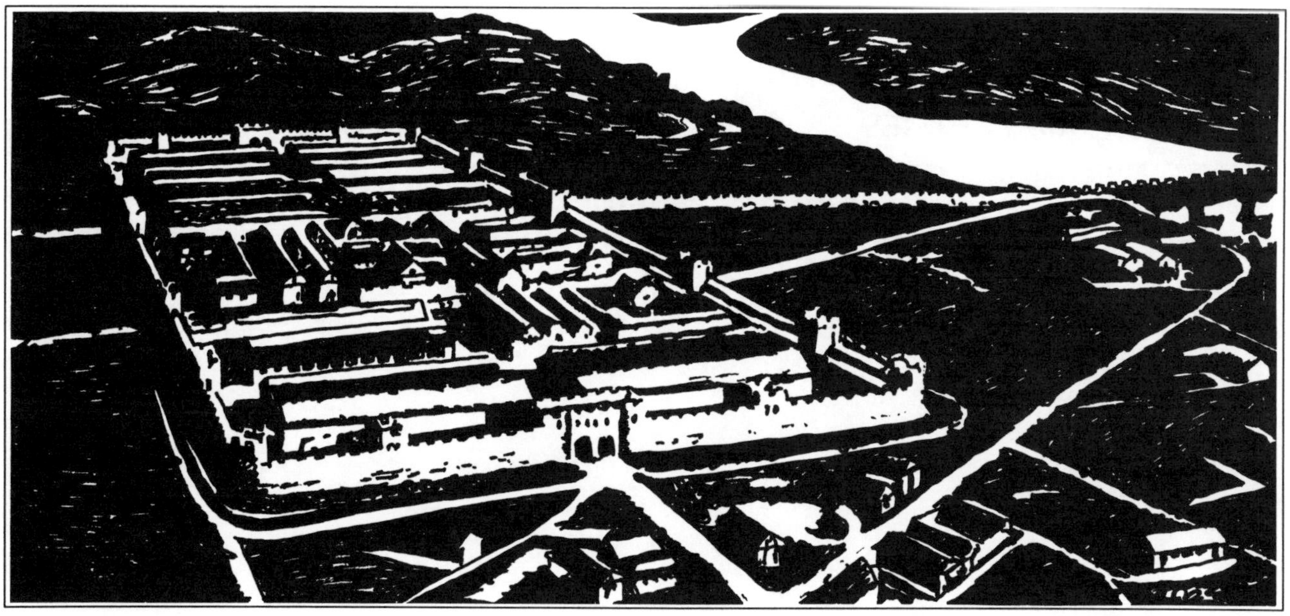

A reconstruction of Chesters Fort

THINK ABOUT

- Whether you are going to build a milecastle or a fort.
- Will it be quicker if you work with a small group of people?
- Will you need cardboard, glue, scissors and paint?
- Who is going to be responsible for each section of the model?
- Protecting the surface you are working on with newspaper.
- Finding a display area.
- Using Unit 11 from *The Roman Empire* to find out more about Roman forts. Some of your writing could be displayed with your model.

PHOTOCOPIABLE

12. TOWN AND COUNTRY LIFE

The street scene shown on page 25 is a reconstruction of the town of Pompeii in Italy. On 24th August 79 AD the town of Pompeii and everyone who lived there was engulfed by the volcanic ash and fumes from a volcano called Vesuvius.

The ash preserved the buildings and these have now been excavated.

NOW

- Look carefully at the reconstructed Roman street on page 25.
- Working with a partner, describe the street in detail.
- Then complete the following activities:
  - Make a list of the different goods on sale in the shops.
  - Explain why you think stone has been used to build the road.
  - What sort of transport can you see?
  - What materials have been used to make containers?
  - Describe any games which you can see being played.
  - Make a drawing of a rich man. Explain why you think he is wealthy.
  - Make a drawing of a poor man. What are the differences between the rich and the poor man?
  - Make a sketch of how women dressed at that time.
- This is a reconstruction of a town, but there are many links with the countryside. Explain how farming is linked to this scene.
- Using the diagram below, make a list of everything which is similar to today. In the second column make a list of everything which is different to today.

SIMILARITIES	DIFFERENCES

13. A ROMAN VILLA

You are going to produce a project about Roman villas.

THINK ABOUT

- Spending a few minutes writing down questions you want to investigate in your project. For example you might want to answer the following:
  - What did a Roman villa look like?
  - What material was used to build it?
  - How did people live in the villa?
  - What sort of furniture was inside?
- Spending some time looking again at Unit 13 in *The Roman Empire* and the information on these pages.
- How you will present your project. For example:
  - in your exercise book.
  - as a wall poster.
  - as a magazine or newspaper.
- Including written work, drawings, plans and diagrams.
- Working with a small group of friends.
- Checking that you have answered the questions you wrote down at the beginning.
- Displaying your project to the rest of the class. You could ask a friend to say what they think is good about it and what they think would have improved it.

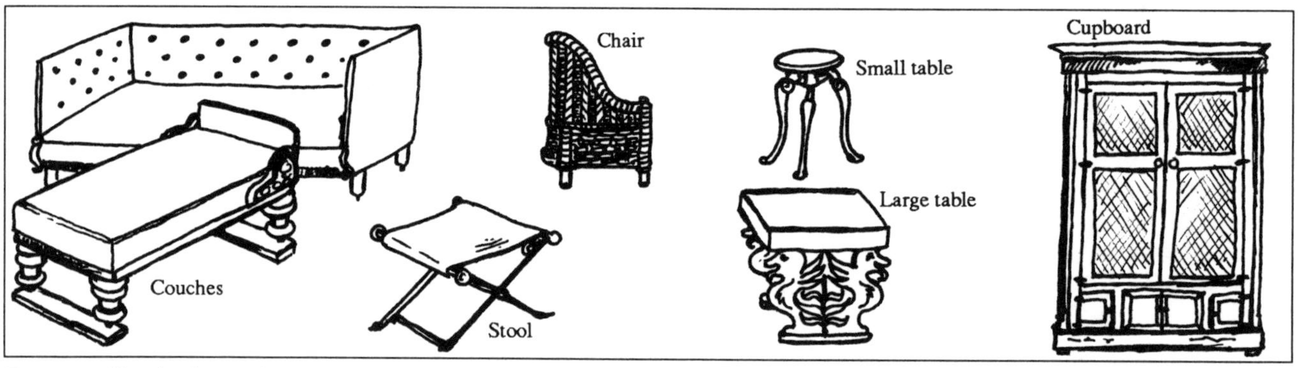

Roman villas had very little furniture. The most important were the couches ,which were used for reclining when eating. Mattresses laid on the floor were usually used for sleeping.

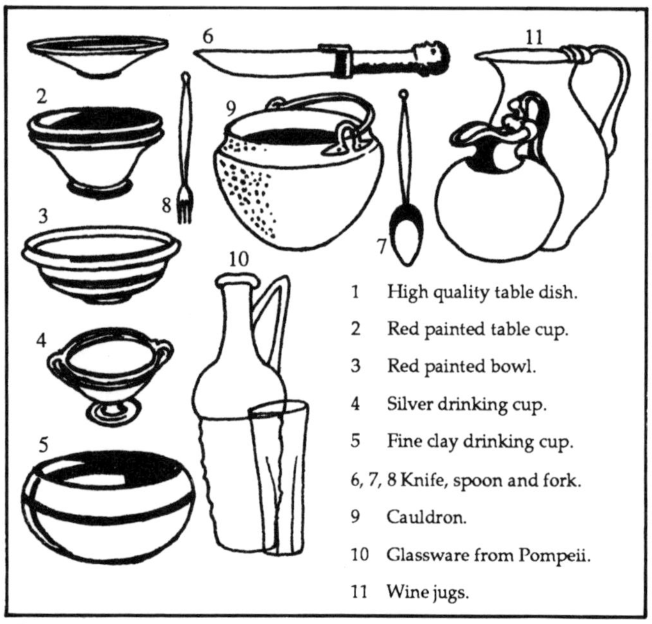

Eating equipment

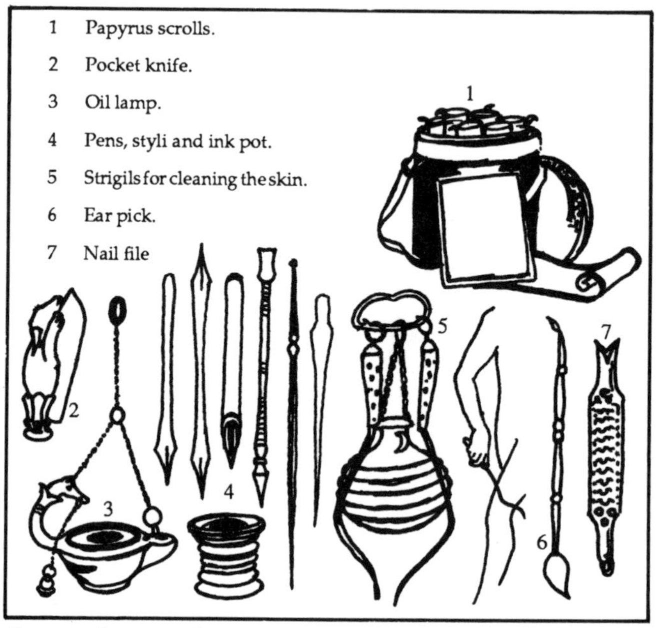

Personal possessions

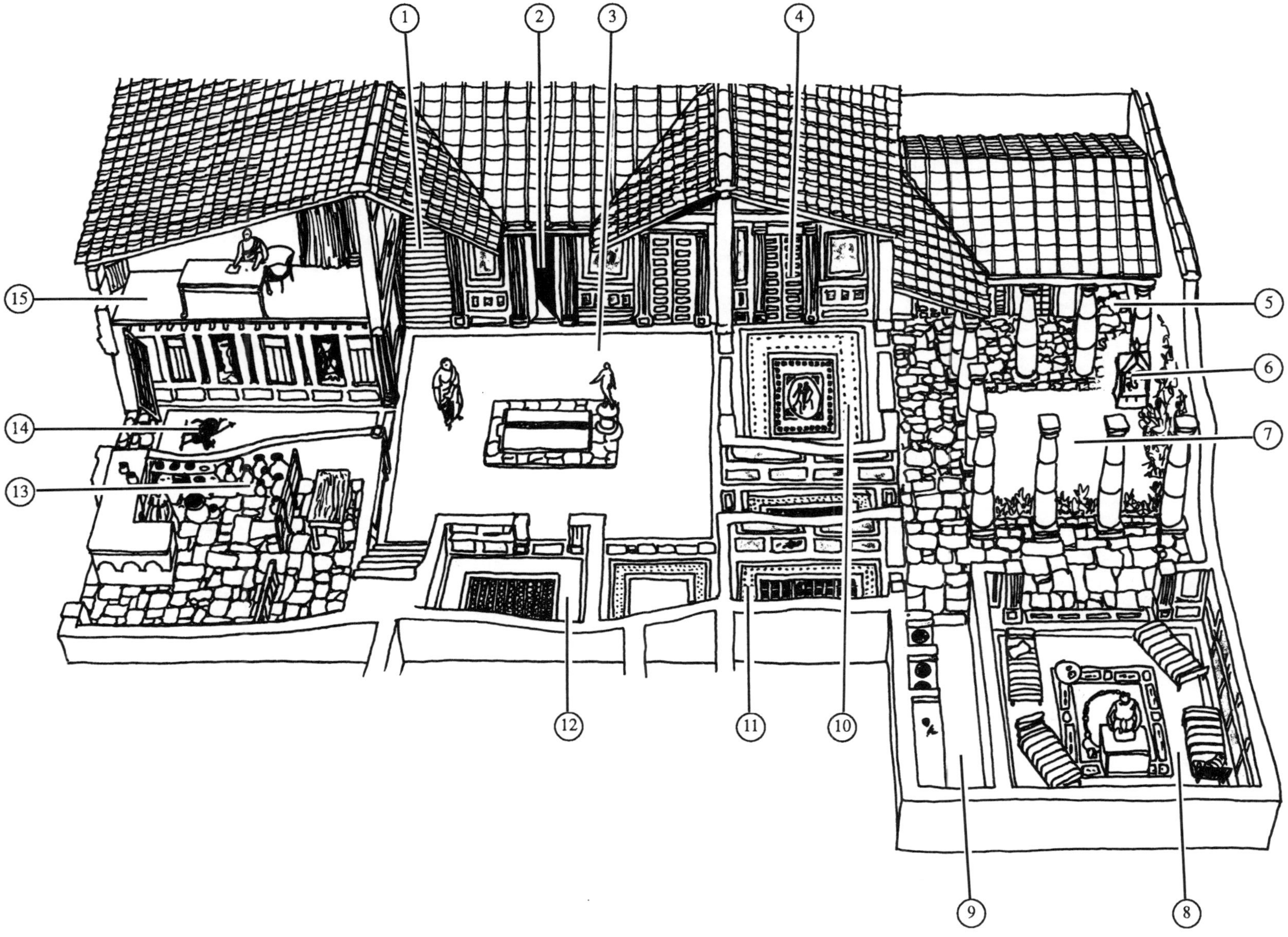

Exploded diagram of a Roman villa

1. Stairs leading to bedroom.

2. Door to bedroom.

3. *Atrium* or main living room. There was an opening in the roof above the pool.

4. Door to a bedroom.

5. The *peristyle*. This was a covered passage around an open courtyard.

6. The *lararium*, the shrine of the household gods.

7. The courtyard of the peristyle bordered by flowerbeds and shrubs. Archaeologists found seeds from some of the original plants when they were excavating Pompeii.

8. The *triclinium* or dining room. The *triclinium* was usually small. It contained three or four couches on which the diners would lie, leaving very little room for the slaves who waited on them.

9. The kitchen. The fuel burned in the ovens was wood or charcoal.

10. The *tablinium*, a reception room or study.

11 and 12. Bedrooms.

13. A shop. The owner of the villa let his spare rooms to shopkeepers. There was another shop on the other side of the entrance passage.

14. In the entrance passage there was a mosaic sign on the floor, *Cave Canem*, which means Beware of the Dog.

15. An upper room, which would probably have been let as a shop. There would have been a separate entrance from the street.

14. ROMAN ENGINEERS

Use this material to help with the Extension Activities of Unit 14 *The Roman Empire*.

A reconstruction of the building of an aqueduct.
Tree trunks are being used to stop the sides caving in. These will be buried once the stone aqueduct is complete.

Cross section of aqueduct.

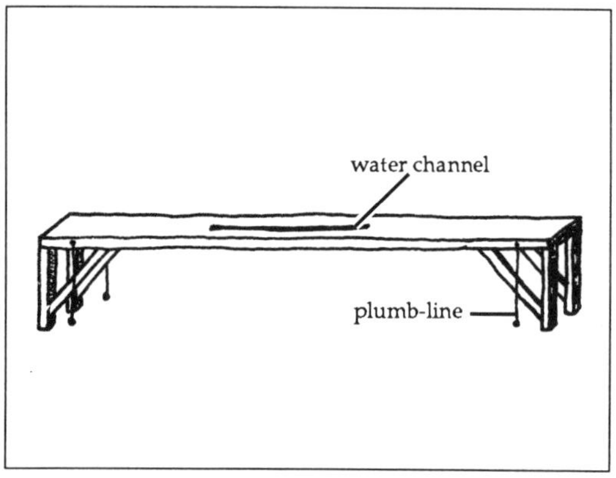

The chorobates was a long narrow table. It was used to check whether the aqueduct was level or sloping correctly.

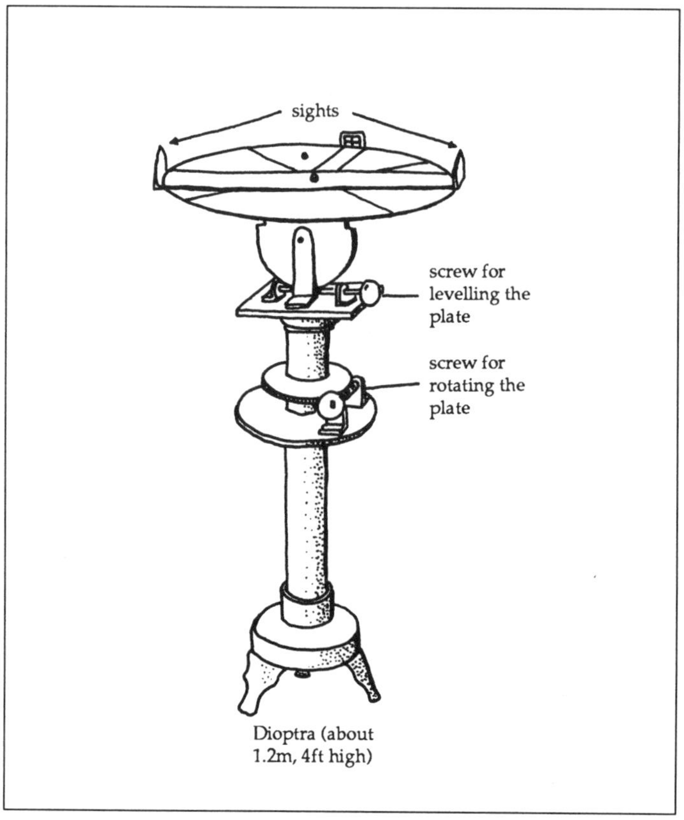

A dioptra was used to take measurements when the aqueduct was being planned. The engineer needed to know the difference in height of the source of the water compared to the city to where it was being piped.

Bridge building
Reconstruction of the building of a bridge

Scaffolding was built on stones which were left projecting.

Building arches

A Roman crane

15. PUBLIC HEALTH

Aim

That pupils should collect information from a video.

Introduction

How to make the best use of video as a teaching/learning medium is a problem often faced by teachers today. These notes detail one method and provide further ideas for use with other videos.

Resources

Video equipment and monitor; *BBC Medicine Through Time Programme 2 'Public Health'*. (Use from the beginning of the programme to the collapse of the Roman Empire - about 10 minutes.)

Organisation

Divide the pupils into five groups. Each group is going to collect information for a particular category. These are: 1. Diseases; 2. Baths; 3. Aqueducts; 4. Sewers; 5. Why the Romans could organise Public Health. The easiest way of dividing pupils into groups is to number the pupils from 1 - 5 round the group. All those given number 1 collect information about diseases; those numbered 2 collect information about baths and so on.

Approach

▼ It should be explained to pupils that each of the five groups will be collecting information related to the category they have been allocated.

▼ Pupils should make brief notes about their category.

▼ The part of the video dealing with the Romans should be watched twice. First time through, pupils do not make notes. Second time, they do.

Follow-up Work

After the video pupils move around the room collecting information from other pupils. At the end of this session everyone should have a complete set of notes on the video.

Advantages

This exercise leads to more purposeful watching of video. As information for only one category is being collected, no one should have to make long notes and so miss most of the video! The follow-up session in which everyone is collecting information from others leads to good motivation and aids cooperative learning.

Further Work

Further suggestions for use of video
The following ideas can be applied to any video programme which schools have available for their history studies.

- *Ask each group of pupils to watch the video from the perspective of one character in the programme. They can decide how the events shown might have affected that character and why the character behaved as he/she did. This approach is useful for developing the concepts of motivation, causation and viewpoints.*
- *Ask pupils to list the different types of evidence shown in the programme. They could then assess the reliability or usefulness of the evidence to historians.*
- *Again splitting pupils into groups; one group could collect information about change, another group about similarities and differences.*

16. LIFE IN ROME

NOW

- Working with a partner, read through all the sources given below.
- Discuss any words you do not understand and ask your teacher if you need any help.
- Get a copy of your 'How do we Know?' sheet.
- Read all the statements carefully.
- Using the sources below, decide whether each statement is true or false.
- Write True or False in the correct column.
- Provide a short quotation from the sources below to prove whether the statement is true or false.

Source 1

For 441 years after the foundation (beginning) of the city, Romans were satisfied to use water from the Tiber and nearby wells or springs. But now 9 aqueducts bring water into the city.

The Aqueducts of Rome Prologue and Book 1.

Source 2

I live over the public baths - you know what that means. Ugh! It's sickening. First there are the strong men doing their exercises and swinging heavy lead weights about with grunts and groans. Next there are the lazy ones having a cheap massage... and what about the ones who leap into the pool making a huge splash as they hit the water.

Lucius Seneca 63AD

Source 3

There's no peace and quiet in the city for a poor man. Early in the morning schoolmasters stop us from having any normal life. Before it gets light we have the bakers, then it's the hammering of the coppersmiths all day.

Marcus Valerius Martial c 40 - 104 AD

Source 4

Vacerra dallies (stays) for hours and sits for a whole day in the latrines (toilets). His real business is to get an invitation to dinner.

Martial c 40 - 104 AD

Source 5

We think ourselves poor if our walls are not covered with huge mirrors ... and our swimming pools lined with marble, and if the water does not pour from silver spouts! And I am talking only about the baths of the common people!

From a letter written at the time.

Source 6

Two of my buildings have collapsed and in the others the walls are all cracked. Not only the tenants but the mice have left!

Marcus Cicero 106 - 43 BC

Source 7

Shops in Rome opened early in the morning and closed at midday. They opened again later... There were barbers, booksellers, grocers, bakers, poultry-sellers, furniture shops and stalls selling cooked-meat.

From a modern history book.

PHOTOCOPIABLE

HOW DO WE KNOW?

STATEMENT	TRUE/FALSE	SUPPORTING EVIDENCE
A. At first Romans used water from the river Tiber.		
B. People only went to the baths to bathe.		
C. Shops in Rome stayed open all day.		
D. There were coppersmiths in Rome.		
E. People visited the public toilets in Rome for many reasons.		
F. The baths for the common people were very plain.		
G. There were many different types of shop in Rome.		
H. All Roman buildings were well built.		
I. Schools began very late in the day.		
J. Romans liked to keep themselves fit.		

Below is a large reconstruction of how the centre of Rome might have looked.

NOW

- Use the reconstruction to find where many of the buildings mentioned in Unit 17 were placed.
- You can also find many examples of the engineering mentioned in Unit 14.

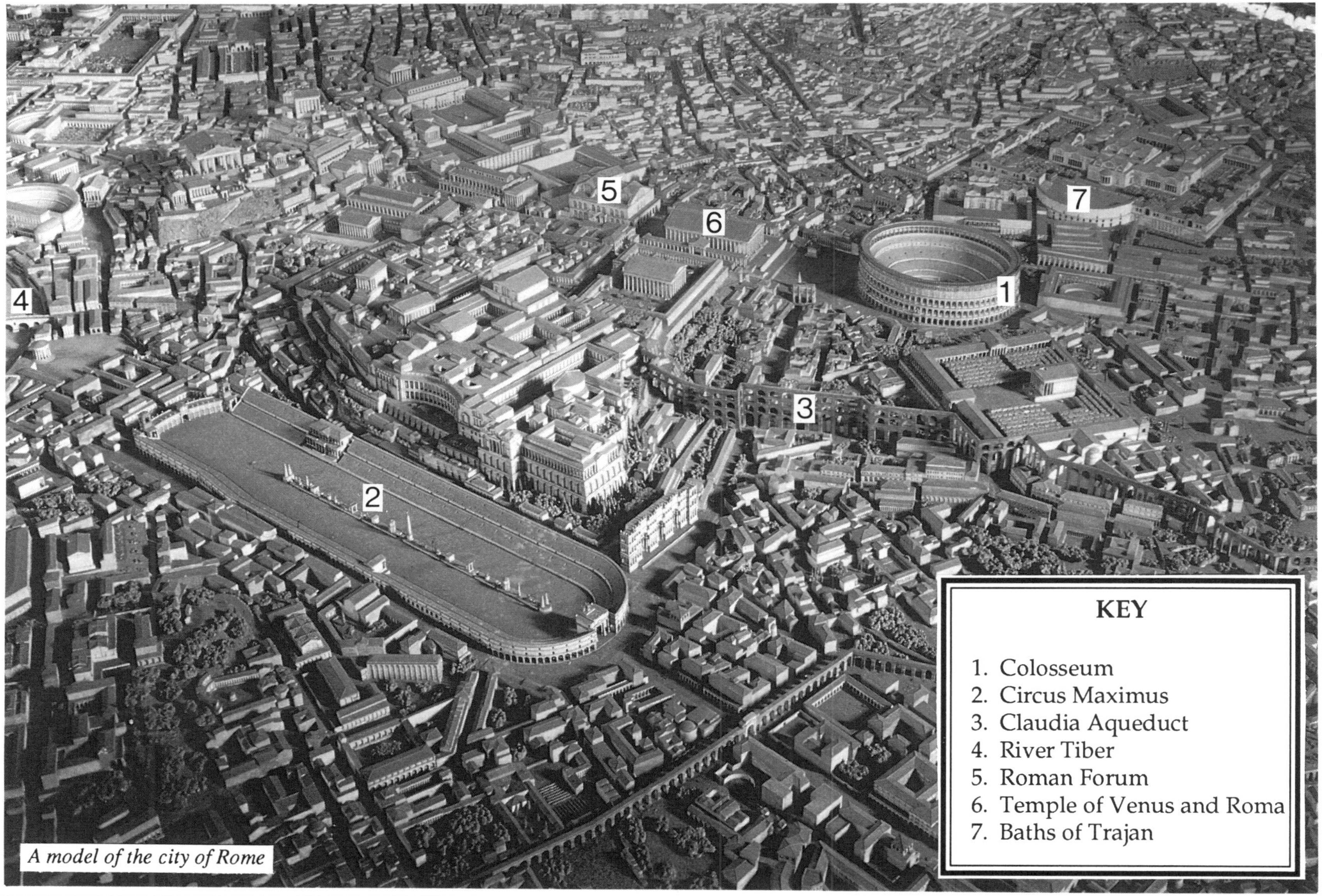

A model of the city of Rome

18. CHILDREN AND THE FAMILY

You have already learnt about the way in which Roman soldiers dressed. In this unit you can learn about the everyday dress of Romans.

Fabric

Most clothing was made from wool or linen. This could be dyed green, red, brown or yellow. Leaves, berries and roots were used as dyes. Purple could only be worn by very important people and boys under 16 years who came from important, high-born families. The purple dye came from a sea shell called the Murex.

The Tunic (tunica)

This was the item of clothing worn by poor and wealthy people.

How to make a tunic

- Use 2 pieces of material big enough to cover your body. If you are a girl then your tunic should almost reach your ankles.
- Stitch across one narrow edge. Then cut a round hole for your head.
- Now stitch up the sides, leaving holes for your arms. Leave these holes quite large so you can put on the tunic easily.
- You will need to wear a belt around your waist.
- The full shoulder part will fall over your shoulders to make sleeves.

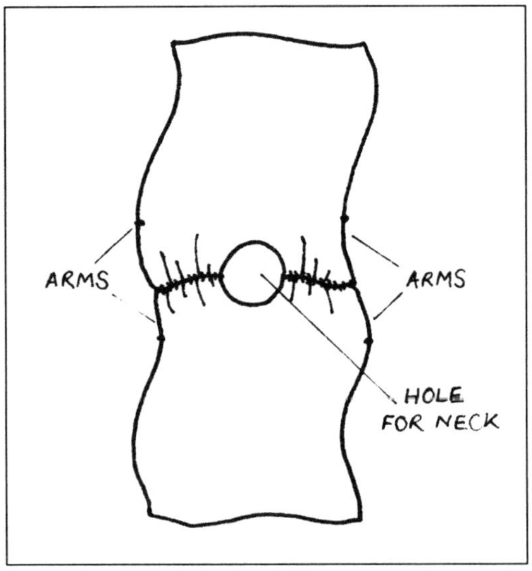

Tunic

A man wearing a tunic

Women's tunics were almost always long. Men wore both long and short tunics.

A woman wearing a tunic

Underwear

Women wore a band of linen as a bra. Both men and women wore underpants. In colder parts of the empire, socks were worn.

The Toga
This was an outdoor garment which was probably very hot when worn in Rome. It was a large piece of material in the shape of a semi-circle and was usually made from wool. The toga was only worn by wealthy men.

The Toga

How to make a toga

- You will need a large piece of semi-circular material. Don't worry if you can't get a piece of cloth as big as that shown in the diagram. An old sheet will do.
- Place the straight edge over your left shoulder, leaving some material hanging down.
- Pull the material under your right arm and throw it back over your left shoulder.
- Now reach under the toga to the piece of material you left hanging down in front of your left leg. Pull it up and tuck it into the belt around your tunic.
  Men would often wear a lightweight cloak instead of the very heavy and warm toga.

The Palla
This was the female version of a toga. It was a piece of fabric which could be worn around the shoulders or over the head.

The Palla

Children's Clothing
Children wore clothing which looked very much like that of the adults.

Shoes
These were usually flat and made from leather.

Boots were also worn. These were made from several layers of leather held together by nails. They were fastened with leather straps.

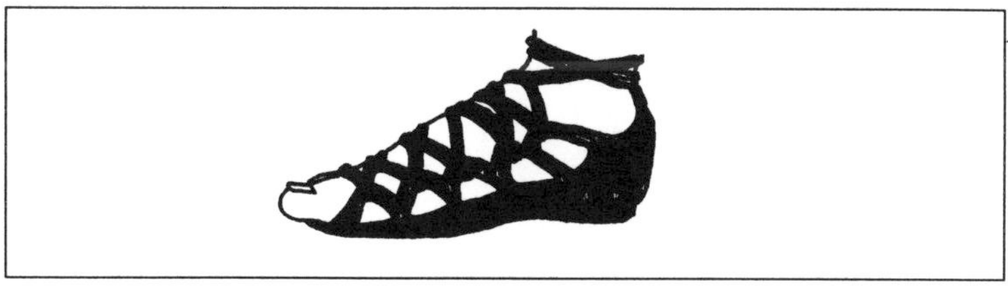
A Roman sandal

See if you can make some of the clothing described in this unit. You could all wear your Roman clothes and act out a street scene like that shown in Unit 12 of this book.

19. EDUCATION - ROMAN WRITING

We have learnt a lot about the Romans from the writing which they left behind. Some of this is written on soft material like linen, papyrus, animal skins and wood. A lot of this writing must have been lost because these soft materials quickly rot away. However, the Romans also wrote on stone. A great deal of this writing has been found by archaeologists digging up Roman remains.

On page 37 you can see some Roman inscriptions from tombstones. Translating inscriptions is really like breaking a code. If you use the information below, you should be able to translate the inscriptions into English.

How to Break the Code

Look carefully at the inscriptions. The **small black triangle** between letters means that the word has been shortened.

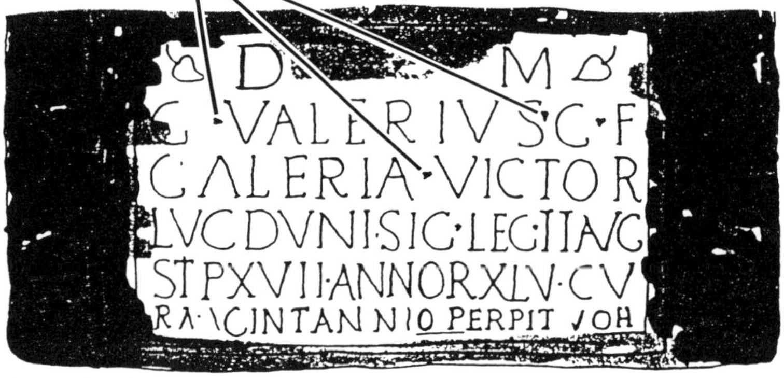

READ

- Roman names.
  Most Roman citizens had 3 names. The first name is usually shortened: for example Mar. for Marcus. Often only the first letter is given of the name: for example T. for Titus. The second name of a man almost always ends in IVS. Often the third name is not used.
  - Look at the inscriptions and find the second names which are given.

- The age the person had reached when they died is usually written: AN or ANN or ANNORVM and followed by the age in Roman numbers.
  CLUE TO SUCCESS: Look back at Unit 19, Education in the Roman Empire, and find the list of Roman numbers.
  - Look at the inscriptions and find the age of the people.

- The number of years the soldier had been in the army. This is usually shown by the letters STIP followed by numbers.
  - Can you find how long some of these people had been in the army?

- The legion to which the soldier had belonged. This is shown by LEG or LEGIO followed by Roman numbers.
  - Can you discover which legion some of these people had been in?

- More information.
  ILIVS means 'son of'.
  CIVIS means 'citizen of' ... This is followed by the name of the person's community.
  BEN means an 'assistant to the governor'.
  MIL means 'a soldier'.
  SIGN or AQVILIF means 'a standard bearer' - someone who carried the flag or sign of the legion.
  FRATER means 'brother'.
  H.S.E. means 'Here lies'.
  HEREDES means 'heirs'.

NOW

* Using all this information, see if you can write out the inscriptions shown below.
* One inscription does not belong to a soldier. Can you identify this inscription?
* What have you been able to learn about how long people lived from these inscriptions?
* List the different ages at which these men joined the army.

Inscriptions on tombstones

20. RELIGION AND CHRISTIANITY

AIM

Use the pages in this unit to help you produce a television programme.

Research

- Read Unit 20 in *The Roman Empire* carefully and complete the Core Activities section.
- Watch an interview on television. The news often uses interviews. Watch carefully how people stand or sit in the studio and for on-the-spot reports. Listen to the sort of questions the interviewer asks. For example you should not ask a question which can be answered with a 'yes' or 'no'. Your questions should be designed to get the other person talking!
- Watch the camera work. Notice that the picture is steady and that the camera moves smoothly from one item to the next.
- Ask your teacher if you can use the school video camera.
- Ask your teacher to help you organise a television studio in a suitable room.

ACTIVITY

- Now find 5 or 6 other people with whom to work.
- You will need the following characters for your programme:
  a presenter; a Roman citizen; another Roman citizen;
  an on-the-spot reporter; Emperor Constantine; interviewer. You will not need a camera person. When everyone's programme is ready, someone from another group can record your programme. Perhaps another group will ask you to record their programme.
- Your group will need to use all the information in Unit 20 of *The Roman Empire.*
- You will need to plan your programme very carefully. On page 39 is a story board. You can use it to help you plan your programme.
- Each person in your group should choose the part they are going to play. Everyone should have a part.
- A script will need to be written for each scene. Every person in that scene should have a copy of the script.
- You could ask your teacher if you can write your script on a word processor, then each person can have a printout.
- Once the script is written, your group should rehearse their programme very carefully. If people can't learn their parts, then the script can be used. Do remember not to hold the script in front of your face!
- If you do not have a video camera then you can just perform your programme for the rest of the class. If you do have a video camera then you will need to set up a television studio.
- Your teacher will show the camera person how to use the camera. You will have to tell the camera person when to move to another scene. It will help if you show your script to the camera person.
- Now record your programme on video.

NOW

- Evaluate your programme with your teacher and the rest of the class. For example you could ask:
  - What people liked about your programme.
  - How it could be improved.
- Talk about what you have learnt from making the programme. It should have helped you remember things better!
- Ask your teacher if the video can be taken home to show your parents.

PHOTOCOPIABLE

THE ROMANS AND CHRISTIANITY

TELEVISION PROGRAMME

Names of Group Members .... ________________ ________________ ________________ ________________	**Scene 1**. A television studio. Character: Presenter seated. **Script** Presenter tells audience what the programme is going to be about.
Scene 2. In the same television studio. Characters: presenter and a Roman citizen called Marcus Sesti. **Script** Presenter asks Marcus Sesti about the gods of the Romans.	**Scene 3**. Same television studio. Character: presenter. **Script** Presenter briefly tells audience about a new religion called Christianity.
Scene 4 In the Roman province of Judea. Characters: interviewer and a Roman woman called Flavia Siculus. **Script** Interviewer asks about the life of Jesus Christ and what Christians believe in.	**Scene 5.** Outside the Colosseum. Character: an on-the-spot reporter. **Script** Reporter describes the deaths of Christians in the arena with lions. Other members of the group will have to provide background noises.
Scene 6. Inside the Senate. Characters: interviewer and Constantine. **Script** Interview with Constantine about his view of Christianity and what he intends to do about the Christians.	**Scene 7.** Back in televison studio. Character: presenter. **Script** Presenter sums up and says goodbye to viewers.

21. THE ARTS

If there had been newspapers in Roman times, below is how the reports on the eruption of Vesuvius might have looked. Some sections have been left blank. You must use the clues in this unit to help you complete each section. Sometimes you need to write, at other times you will need to draw.

THOUSANDS DIE AS VOLCANO ERUPTS

27th August, 79 AD

At 1.00pm on August 24th 79 AD a strange, pine tree shaped cloud appeared in the sky over the towns of Pompeii and Herculaneum. The cloud was very high. Sometimes it seemed dark, at others times it was bright. The cloud carried ash and pumice stone which rained down on the city of Pompeii. Many people suffocated as the ash and stone buried them. Others died as they ran from the city. They had breathed in the poisonous sulphur fumes which the cloud also carried.

Map showing position of Pompeii

As you can see from the map Pompeii is situated . . .

____

____

____

____

____

The Ruins of Pompeii

In this picture you can see how the city was devasted. Notice the . . .

____

____

____

____

____

____

____

____

PHOTOCOPIABLE

For three days the volcano continued to erupt. Flames and smoke could be seen shooting out of the top of Vesuvius. Some people were rescued from their houses. People tied pillows to their heads to protect themselves from falling stones. The cloud kept turning the sky dark. Every time this happened people screamed and prayed to the gods for help. Some people went mad.

Dog

A woman

It is thought that some 2 000 people may have died. In these pictures you can see . . .

____

____

____

The theatres, public baths, temples and public buildings were all covered with about 4 metres of thick dust and stones. The shops in the streets leading to the forum (market place) were also destroyed along with all the goods which were for sale.

This is how Vesuvius looked

A villa in Pompeii

It is thought that because of the poisonous fumes and dust, people will never again be able to live in Pompeii. The 24th August will be a day which is remembered with great sadness. It was the day that a Roman city and its people died.

This is one of the many beautiful villas which were destroyed. In the picture you can see. . .

____

____

____

22. COLLAPSE OF THE EMPIRE

You will remember from Unit 22 in *The Roman Empire* that in 330 AD the emperor Constantine built a new city in the east which became known as Constantinople.

- In this unit you can see drawings of people and places from the city. Look at them carefully.
- In the blank spaces you should explain how things had changed compared with earlier Roman times.
  CLUE TO SUCCESS: Look back through all the units in *The Roman Empire*. Use the contents page and the index at the back of the book to help you find the right sections.
- You can explain the changes by using drawings or writing.

The position of Byzantium and Rome

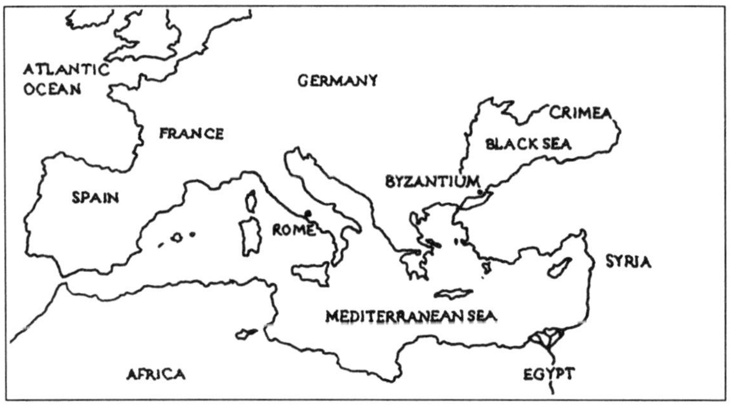

Action Slot 1

* Explain the difference between the position of Rome and the position of Byzantium.

* What sort of changes might the different position have brought about?

The emperor Justinian and the empress Theodora 6th century AD with wealthy people from their court

Action Slot 2

* How has the style of clothing changed since Roman times?

* Have hairstyles changed?

* How has furniture changed?

Working people

Action Slot 3

* How has the style of clothing for working people changed?

Soldiers

Action Slot 4

* Explain the differences between these soldiers from Byzantium and those of Rome.

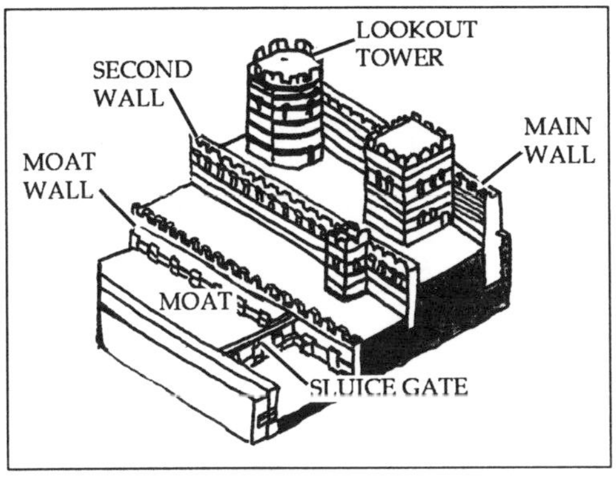

The city walls of Byzantium

Action Slot 5

* Find other walls built by the Romans and explain the differences.

Architecture

This is the church of St. Sophia, built in 537 AD.

Action Slot 6

* Make a list of all the differences between this church and Roman temples.

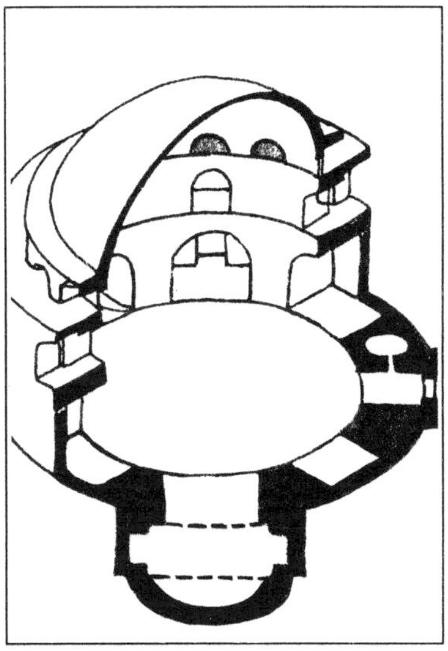

Style of churches

Action Slot 7

* Can you identify any differences between these ships from Byzantium and those used by Romans?

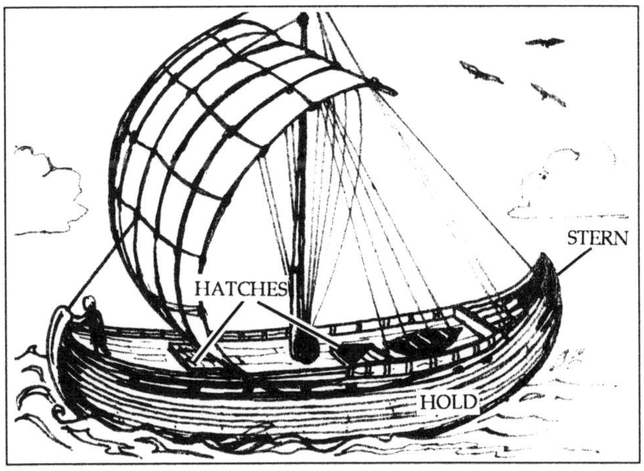

Cargo ships

PHOTOCOPIABLE

23. THE LEGACY OF ROME

You should identify some of the Roman ideas which have influenced our lives today.

NOW

- You should do this exercise before you work through Unit 23 in *The Roman Empire.*
- Your teacher will give you a pack of cards.
- Working with a partner, place the cards face downwards on a desk or table.
- Take it in turns to turn over a card.
- When a card is turned over, find the number on the chart below.
- In the column headed CAPTION write the name of the object shown on the card.
- Write the connection with life today in the column headed LINKS WITH TODAY.
- Continue in this way until you have worked through all the cards.

NUMBER	CAPTION	LINKS WITH TODAY
1		
2		
3		
4		
5		
6		
7		
8		
9		
10		
11		
12		
13		
14		
15		
16		

1

DE BRITANN

2

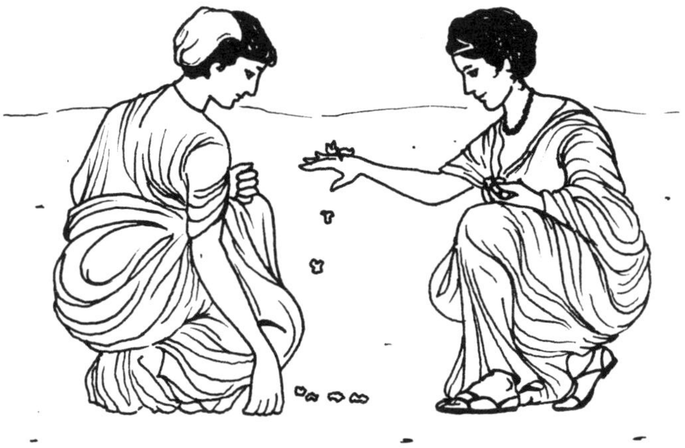

3

4

5

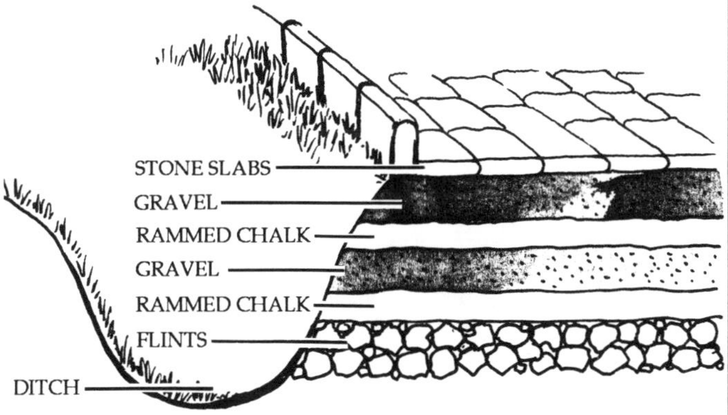
STONE SLABS
GRAVEL
RAMMED CHALK
GRAVEL
RAMMED CHALK
FLINTS
DITCH

6

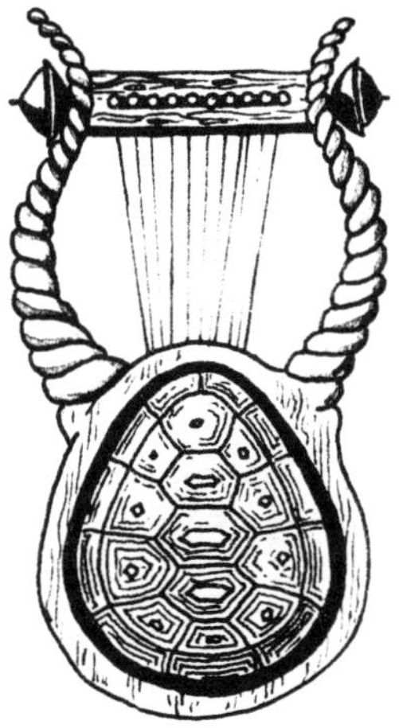

7

8

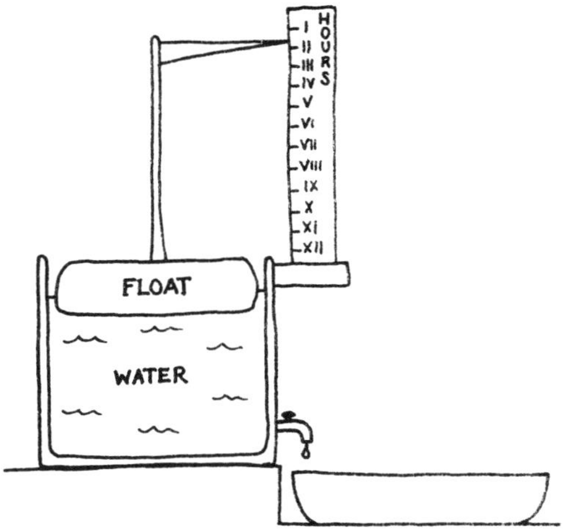
HOURS
I
II
III
IV
V
VI
VII
VIII
IX
X
XI
XII
FLOAT
WATER

9

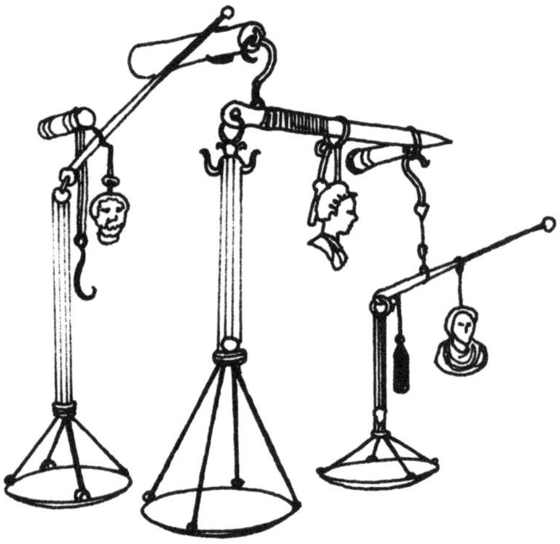

10

11

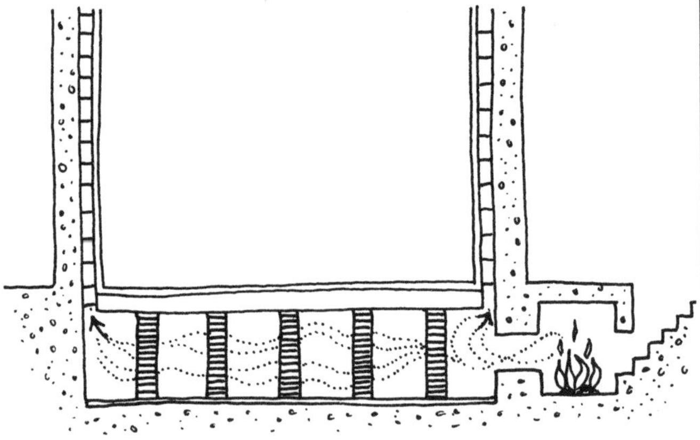

12

13

14

15

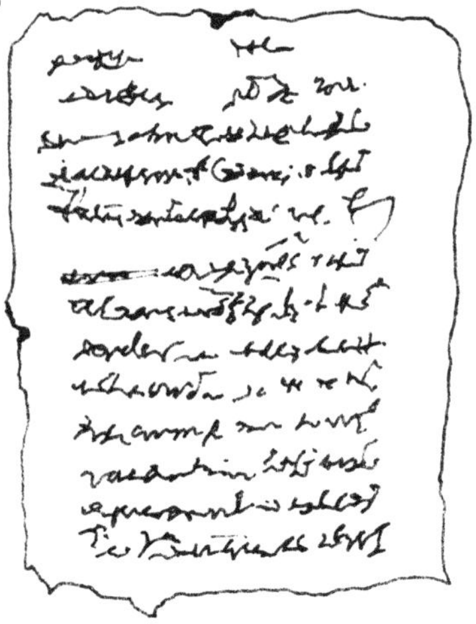

I II III

IV V VI

VII VIII IX

X

16

Janus	Julius
Februa	Augustus
Mars	Septem
Aphrilis	Octo
Maia	Novem
Juno	Decem

PHOTOCOPIABLE

THE NATIONAL CURRICULUM

A matrix is provided below in order that teachers may identify where *The Roman Empire* and the accompanying teacher-resource book fulfil attainment targets of the National Curriculum.

	AT1	AT2	AT3
The Roman Empire 1	●		
2	●		●
3	●		
4	●		●
5	●	●	
6	●	●	●
7	●		●
8	●		●
9	●		●
10	●		
11	●		●
12	●		
13	●		●
14	●	●	●
15	●	●	
16	●	●	
17	●	●	
18	●		
19	●		●
20	●		
21	●		●
22	●		
23	●		

	AT1	AT2	AT3
Resource Book 1	●		
2	●		
3	●		●
4	●		●
5	●		
6	●		
7	●	●	
8	●		
9	●		
10	●		●
11	●		
12	●	●	
13	●		
14	●		
15	●		
16	●		●
17	●		
18	●		
19	●		●
20	●		●
21	●		
22	●		
23	●		●

PHOTOCOPIABLE

Self Assessment Sheet of Historical Skills

Name .... **Group or class ....**

Concept	Skill	Pupil	Teacher
Evidence	● can identify primary and secondary evidence ● can name 6 different types of evidence ● can ask questions about evidence ● can interpret pictorial evidence ● can interpret written evidence ● can interpret an artefact ● can collect oral evidence ● can record the details of a site on a labelled sketch ● can draw a simple plan of a site ● can raise questions about a site ● can explain problems connected with - written evidence - pictorial evidence - artefacts - oral evidence - maps - buildings		
Chronology	● can place evidence in chronological order ● can place events in chronological sequence ● can draw a simple time-line ● can place a given year in the correct century		
Empathy	● can demonstrate an understanding of different viewpoints ● can describe how people might have felt		
Change and continuity	● can recognise and describe change ● can recognise and describe continuity		

